Immersive Reader

The Microsoft 365 Companion Series

Dr. Patrick Jones

OLYMPUS ACADEMY
PRESS

Copyright © 2024 by Patrick Jones

All rights reserved, including the right to reproduce this book or portions thereof in any form.

TABLE OF CONTENTS

Empowering Comprehension and Accessibility 1

What is Microsoft Immersive Reader? 5

Why Use Microsoft Immersive Reader? 9

Getting Started with Microsoft Immersive Reader 15

Best Practices for Microsoft Immersive Reader 21

Tips and Tricks for Microsoft Immersive Reader 27

A Smarter Way to Read and Understand 33

Common Pitfalls and How to Avoid Them 37

Sarah's Journey with Immersive Reader 43

Immersive Reader and Your Journey 47

Unlocking Your Potential with Immersive Reader 51

EMPOWERING COMPREHENSION AND ACCESSIBILITY

Imagine a tool that transforms the way we read, making text more accessible, engaging, and personalized. Microsoft Immersive Reader is precisely that—a groundbreaking feature designed to empower users of all ages and abilities to read with confidence and comprehension. Whether you're a student striving to master complex material, a professional looking to improve focus, or someone with unique reading needs, Immersive Reader creates an environment where text becomes approachable and understandable.

In a world where information flows faster than ever, being able to process and comprehend text efficiently is a vital skill. Immersive Reader levels the playing field, offering features that support readers of all abilities by tailoring text to their unique needs. From adjusting text size and spacing to breaking down syllables and translating words, this tool redefines what it means to make content accessible.

For many, reading can be a challenge. Dyslexia, ADHD, language barriers, or simply navigating dense text can hinder comprehension and slow productivity. Immersive Reader removes these barriers by offering a suite of features designed to make reading effortless and enjoyable.

With Immersive Reader, you can:

- Adjust text for better readability by changing font size, spacing, and background color.
- Use tools like Read Aloud to hear text spoken aloud at your preferred pace.
- Translate words or entire passages into different languages, making content globally accessible.

- Highlight parts of speech or syllables for deeper language understanding.

Immersive Reader isn't just for those with challenges; it's for anyone looking to improve their reading experience.

This book is your guide to mastering Immersive Reader, understanding its features, and using it to transform the way you interact with text. Inside, you'll discover:

- What Immersive Reader is and why it's a revolutionary tool for accessibility and comprehension.
- How to get started with Immersive Reader in Microsoft tools like Word, OneNote, Teams, and beyond.
- Best practices for using Immersive Reader to enhance learning, focus, and productivity.
- Tips and tricks to customize your reading experience for maximum benefit.
- How Copilot, Microsoft's AI assistant, integrates with Immersive Reader to provide personalized reading support.
- Real-world applications through Sarah's journey as she uses Immersive Reader to overcome her own challenges and help her team thrive.

In this book, we'll follow Sarah, a marketing professional who initially struggles to process dense reports and communicate with a global team. Discovering Immersive Reader becomes a turning point for her, not only helping her focus and understand material but also enabling her to collaborate with colleagues from diverse linguistic backgrounds.

Written in a conversational and approachable style, this book simplifies the complexities of Immersive Reader, ensuring that even the most technical features feel accessible. Whether you're exploring this tool for yourself, your students, or your team, this guide is designed to inspire confidence and unlock new possibilities for comprehension and productivity.

As you turn the pages, you'll uncover the transformative power of Microsoft Immersive Reader. By the end, you'll not only understand how to use its features but also feel equipped to harness its potential for greater comprehension, learning, and collaboration. Let's embark on this journey of empowerment and discovery together!

WHAT IS MICROSOFT IMMERSIVE READER?

Microsoft Immersive Reader is a transformative tool designed to make reading more accessible and engaging for everyone. Built with inclusivity in mind, it's not just a reading aid but a gateway to understanding, collaboration, and learning. Whether you're navigating dense documents, learning a new language, or supporting students with unique learning needs, Immersive Reader adapts to your requirements, creating a personalized reading experience.

At its core, Immersive Reader is about breaking down barriers. It's a feature designed to support users with diverse needs, from students with dyslexia to professionals juggling multilingual communications. Yet, its appeal isn't limited to those with challenges—anyone looking to improve focus, comprehension, or productivity can benefit from its features.

With Immersive Reader, Microsoft has reimagined how text is consumed by focusing on three pillars: accessibility, engagement, and understanding.

Key Features of Immersive Reader

1. **Text Customization**
   Immersive Reader allows users to modify text appearance to suit their preferences, ensuring maximum readability.
   - Adjust text size, font, and spacing for clarity.
   - Change the background color to reduce visual strain, with options like sepia and dark mode.
   - Enable line focus, which highlights one line at a time to enhance concentration.

2. **Language and Translation Support**
   Bridging language barriers, Immersive Reader offers robust translation tools.
   - Translate individual words or entire passages into over 60 languages.
   - Hear translations read aloud for better pronunciation and comprehension.

3. **Reading Aloud**
   Sometimes hearing text can make it easier to process. Immersive Reader's Read Aloud feature:
   - Converts written text into speech, allowing users to listen at their preferred pace.
   - Offers adjustable voice speed and tone for a personalized experience.

4. **Grammar Tools**
   For language learners or those analyzing text, Immersive Reader includes:
   - Syllable splitting to break down complex words.
   - Highlighting parts of speech, such as nouns, verbs, and adjectives, in different colors.

5. **Picture Dictionary**
   The Picture Dictionary provides visual representations of words, helping users grasp meaning quickly, especially in educational settings or for language learners.

Immersive Reader is seamlessly integrated across various Microsoft tools, making it accessible no matter where you work or learn:

- **Word:** Simplify complex documents and make editing easier.
- **OneNote:** Enhance note-taking and studying.
- **Teams:** Improve communication and accessibility during chats and meetings.
- **Outlook:** Read emails with clarity and focus.
- **Edge Browser:** Use Immersive Reader to simplify web pages and remove distractions.

Example: Sarah discovered Immersive Reader in Teams while reviewing project updates from her global colleagues. With translation and Read Aloud features, she could understand multilingual notes and focus on key takeaways effortlessly.

Immersive Reader isn't just a convenience—it's a tool that fosters inclusion and equity. By catering to diverse needs, it ensures that everyone has an equal opportunity to learn, collaborate, and thrive.

For students, it's a bridge to deeper understanding. For professionals, it's a productivity enhancer. For educators, it's a teaching companion. No matter the context, Immersive Reader empowers users to interact with text in ways that suit them best.

WHY USE MICROSOFT IMMERSIVE READER?

In a world overflowing with information, being able to read, understand, and engage with text is essential for learning, productivity, and collaboration. However, not everyone processes information the same way. Challenges like dyslexia, ADHD, visual impairments, or even language barriers can make reading more difficult. Microsoft Immersive Reader addresses these issues head-on, providing tools that empower users to customize their reading experience, break down language barriers, and improve focus and comprehension.

But Immersive Reader isn't just for those with challenges—it's for anyone who wants to engage with text more effectively. Whether you're a student trying to master a subject, a teacher aiming to reach every learner, or a professional juggling complex documents, Immersive Reader offers benefits that make reading a more inclusive and enjoyable experience.

1. Accessibility for All

Why It Matters:
Not everyone reads text in the same way. People with dyslexia, visual impairments, or other reading challenges often struggle to keep up in environments where written communication is dominant. Immersive Reader provides features that make text more accessible and adaptable to individual needs.

How It Helps:

- Adjustable text size, spacing, and background colors reduce visual strain.
- Read Aloud offers auditory support for users who process information better when they hear it.

- Line focus helps users maintain their place while reading long passages.

Example: Sarah's colleague, who has dyslexia, used Immersive Reader to adjust text spacing and enable Read Aloud during a team presentation. This allowed them to follow along and contribute more confidently.

2. Enhancing Focus and Comprehension

Why It Matters:
In today's fast-paced world, distractions are everywhere. Staying focused on dense or complex text can be challenging even for the most adept readers.

How It Helps:

- Line focus minimizes distractions by highlighting one line at a time.
- Breaking words into syllables aids language learners and readers processing unfamiliar terms.
- Highlighting parts of speech (nouns, verbs, adjectives) improves comprehension for learners analyzing language structure.

Example: During a hectic workday, Sarah used Immersive Reader's line focus feature to read through a lengthy report. By reducing visual clutter, she quickly identified the key takeaways and moved on to her next task with confidence.

3. Bridging Language Barriers

Why It Matters:
Language is no longer a barrier to collaboration in global teams or multicultural classrooms. Immersive Reader's translation tools enable users to work across languages seamlessly.

How It Helps:

- Translates individual words or entire passages into over 60 languages.
- Provides spoken pronunciation of translated text to aid communication.

Example: Sarah's team included members from several countries. Using Immersive Reader's translation feature, she converted an English document into Spanish for her colleagues, ensuring that everyone could participate equally.

4. Empowering Education

Why It Matters:
Teachers face the challenge of addressing diverse learning needs in their classrooms. Immersive Reader equips educators with tools to support every student, whether they're visual learners, struggling readers, or advanced language learners.

How It Helps:

- Picture Dictionary enables young readers or ESL students to understand words visually.
- Grammar tools break down text, highlighting parts of speech to reinforce language skills.
- Read Aloud fosters independence by letting students hear the text as they follow along.

Example: Sarah's friend, a teacher, used Immersive Reader in her classroom to help students with varying literacy levels engage with a shared reading assignment. Students could adjust the tool to fit their needs, making the lesson accessible and inclusive.

5. Boosting Productivity in the Workplace

Why It Matters:
Professionals often deal with dense documents, tight deadlines, and the need to collaborate with diverse teams. Immersive Reader simplifies these challenges by enhancing understanding and streamlining communication.

How It Helps:

- Read Aloud accelerates comprehension of long reports during time crunches.
- Line focus and adjustable text features improve clarity during review.
- Translation tools facilitate smoother communication with international colleagues.

Example: While preparing for a client presentation, Sarah used Immersive Reader to simplify and proofread her content, ensuring that her key points were clear and impactful.

6. Encouraging Lifelong Learning

Why It Matters:
Immersive Reader doesn't just support reading—it encourages growth. By making content accessible and engaging, it empowers users to learn, explore, and communicate with greater confidence.

How It Helps:

- Language learners can practice pronunciation and comprehension with translation and Read Aloud tools.
- Individuals can overcome reading challenges to engage with new information.
- Personalized features create a stress-free reading environment, making learning enjoyable.

Example: Sarah began using Immersive Reader to explore articles in other languages, gradually improving her French comprehension.

Immersive Reader isn't just about accessibility; it's about transformation. It's about giving every individual the tools they need to read, learn, and connect on their terms. By enhancing focus, breaking down barriers, and encouraging exploration, Immersive Reader redefines what's possible for readers of all abilities.

GETTING STARTED WITH MICROSOFT IMMERSIVE READER

Microsoft Immersive Reader is an intuitive and user-friendly tool, but taking your first steps can feel daunting if you're new to its features. This chapter is your guide to navigating Immersive Reader, from where to find it across Microsoft tools to customizing it to suit your unique needs. Whether you're using it for personal growth, professional tasks, or educational purposes, this guide ensures you'll be up and running in no time.

1. Where to Find Immersive Reader

Immersive Reader is seamlessly integrated into various Microsoft tools, making it accessible wherever you work or learn. Here's how to locate it in popular applications:

- **Word:**
  In the web and desktop versions of Word, open a document, then select View > Immersive Reader.

- **OneNote:**
  Open a note, click View > Immersive Reader, and watch your content transform into an interactive, accessible format.

- **Teams:**
  Use Immersive Reader in chats or posts by clicking the three-dot menu next to a message and selecting Immersive Reader.

- **Outlook:**
  Open an email, select the three-dot menu, and click Immersive Reader to simplify the content.

- **Edge Browser:**
  On a webpage, click the Immersive Reader icon in the address bar to declutter and enhance readability.

Pro Tip: If you don't see Immersive Reader, ensure your app or browser is updated to the latest version.

2. Activating Immersive Reader

Once you've located Immersive Reader, activating it is as simple as a few clicks:

1. Open the content you want to read (e.g., a document, note, or email).
2. Click on the Immersive Reader option in the toolbar or menu.
3. Your text will transform into a clean, distraction-free layout, ready for customization.

Example: Sarah activated Immersive Reader in OneNote during a team meeting to review her notes with better focus and clarity.

3. Customizing Your Reading Experience

Immersive Reader offers a variety of settings to tailor the reading experience to your needs. Here's how to customize it:

- **Text Preferences:**
    - Adjust text size, spacing, and font style to improve readability.
    - Change the background color to reduce eye strain with options like sepia or dark mode.
- **Grammar Tools:**
    - Enable syllable splitting to break down complex words.
    - Highlight parts of speech, such as nouns, verbs, and adjectives, in different colors to enhance understanding.
- **Reading Preferences:**

- Use line focus to highlight one, three, or five lines of text at a time.
- Activate the Picture Dictionary to see visual representations of specific words.
- Enable Read Aloud to listen to the text while following along visually.

Pro Tip: Experiment with different settings to find what works best for you.

4. Using Immersive Reader for Translation

Immersive Reader's translation feature is a game-changer for multilingual users. Here's how to use it:

1. Select the Translate option from the menu.
2. Choose a language from the extensive list available.
3. Translate a single word or the entire text.

Example: Sarah translated a client's email from French to English in Outlook, allowing her to respond quickly and accurately.

Pro Tip: Combine translation with Read Aloud to practice pronunciation and comprehension in a new language.

5. Exploring Advanced Features

Immersive Reader goes beyond basic customization with advanced tools that enhance productivity and engagement:

- **Line Focus:**
  Helps maintain concentration by isolating one line or a small group of lines while dimming the rest of the text.

- **Reading Speed Adjustment:**
  Customize Read Aloud's voice speed and tone to match your preferences.
- **Interactive Features:**
  In Teams, use Immersive Reader to simplify and translate chat messages, fostering clearer communication across global teams.

Example: During a project review, Sarah used line focus to dissect a dense technical report, ensuring she didn't miss critical details.

6. Saving and Sharing Content

Immersive Reader integrates seamlessly with Microsoft's cloud-based ecosystem, allowing you to save and share your work effortlessly:

- Save annotated or customized text back to Word, OneNote, or other tools for future reference.
- Share translated or simplified content with colleagues or classmates to improve collaboration.

Example: Sarah customized a OneNote page using Immersive Reader, saved it, and shared the streamlined version with her team for easy review.

7. Accessing Immersive Reader Across Devices

Immersive Reader isn't tied to a single device—it's available wherever you go:

- Use it on your desktop for detailed work.
- Access it on mobile devices for on-the-go reading and learning.
- Sync settings across devices through your Microsoft account for a seamless experience.

Pro Tip: Download the Microsoft apps you use most frequently to ensure Immersive Reader is always at your fingertips.

Now that you've learned how to access and customize Immersive Reader, you're ready to explore its practical applications.

BEST PRACTICES FOR MICROSOFT IMMERSIVE READER

Microsoft Immersive Reader is an exceptional tool for enhancing reading, comprehension, and communication. However, like any tool, its impact is amplified when used thoughtfully and strategically. In this chapter, we'll explore best practices to ensure you make the most of Immersive Reader's powerful features. Whether you're using it in education, the workplace, or for personal growth, these strategies will help you unlock its full potential.

1. Customize the Experience for Your Needs

Why It Matters:
Immersive Reader is designed to adapt to different reading styles and preferences. Taking the time to customize its settings ensures a more comfortable and effective experience.

Best Practices:

- Experiment with text size, spacing, and background color to find what's easiest on your eyes.
- Use line focus to improve concentration during lengthy or dense readings.
- Adjust the Read Aloud speed and voice tone to match your preferred listening pace.

Example: Sarah often struggled to stay focused on dense project reports. By enabling line focus and slowing down the Read Aloud speed, she found it much easier to process key details.

Pro Tip: Save your preferred settings for a consistent experience across devices.

2. Integrate Grammar Tools for Learning

Why It Matters:
Grammar tools like syllable splitting and parts of speech highlighting enhance language comprehension, especially for students and language learners.

Best Practices:

- Highlight nouns, verbs, and adjectives to better understand sentence structure.
- Use syllable splitting to break down complex words and improve pronunciation.
- Combine these tools with Read Aloud for a multisensory learning experience.

Example: A teacher in Sarah's organization used grammar tools during a virtual training session to help employees improve their technical writing skills.

Pro Tip: Pair grammar tools with real-world texts, like emails or reports, to reinforce learning in practical contexts.

3. Leverage Translation Features for Multilingual Collaboration

Why It Matters:
In today's globalized world, effective communication often requires overcoming language barriers. Immersive Reader's translation tools make this easier.

Best Practices:

- Translate entire documents for a comprehensive understanding of the content.
- Use single-word translations to build vocabulary in a new language.

- Share translated content with teammates to improve collaboration.

Example: Sarah's team included members from multiple countries. She used Immersive Reader to translate meeting notes into Spanish and French, ensuring every team member felt included.

Pro Tip: Use Read Aloud in conjunction with translation to practice pronunciation and deepen language comprehension.

4. Utilize Immersive Reader in Microsoft Teams

Why It Matters:
Immersive Reader's integration with Teams improves communication by simplifying chat messages and posts, particularly in busy or multilingual environments.

Best Practices:

- Use Immersive Reader to translate chat messages for clarity during team discussions.
- Enable line focus when reviewing lengthy posts to stay focused.
- Highlight key sections of messages with Read Aloud to ensure nothing is missed.

Example: During a virtual brainstorming session, Sarah used Immersive Reader to simplify a colleague's technical explanation, enabling her to contribute effectively despite not being an expert in the field.

Pro Tip: Encourage team members to use Immersive Reader during meetings to bridge communication gaps.

5. Enhance Educational Experiences

Why It Matters:
Immersive Reader's tools are a boon for educators and learners alike, supporting diverse learning styles and improving classroom inclusivity.

Best Practices:

- Introduce Picture Dictionary to help younger students or language learners understand unfamiliar words.
- Use Read Aloud to engage auditory learners and reinforce reading comprehension.
- Create a distraction-free environment with line focus and customizable text settings.

Example: A teacher in Sarah's network used Immersive Reader to help students with reading difficulties follow along with class materials, boosting their confidence and participation.

Pro Tip: Encourage students to explore Immersive Reader on their own, fostering independence and self-directed learning.

6. Make Complex Content Manageable

Why It Matters:
Complex reports, lengthy articles, and dense documents can be overwhelming. Immersive Reader helps simplify and clarify these texts for easier comprehension.

Best Practices:

- Use Read Aloud to break large sections into manageable chunks.
- Apply translation tools to decode jargon or unfamiliar terms.
- Highlight parts of speech to analyze technical documents more effectively.

Example: Sarah faced a daunting industry whitepaper full of dense terminology. By enabling syllable splitting and using the Picture Dictionary, she was able to grasp the key concepts without feeling overwhelmed.

Pro Tip: Combine Immersive Reader with tools like OneNote for note-taking and summarizing long texts.

7. Save and Share Customized Content

Why It Matters:
Sharing Immersive Reader-enhanced content ensures that everyone, regardless of their reading preferences or challenges, can access and engage with the material.

Best Practices:

- Save customized documents in formats that retain Immersive Reader settings.
- Share simplified or translated content with colleagues or students for improved collaboration.
- Use Immersive Reader during presentations to make content accessible to all participants.

Example: Sarah shared an Immersive Reader-enhanced version of her project notes with her team, ensuring everyone had access to the same clear, organized information.

Pro Tip: Combine Immersive Reader with OneDrive or SharePoint to distribute materials efficiently.

Immersive Reader is more than a tool; it's a bridge to understanding and inclusivity. By applying these best practices, you'll maximize its potential and create an environment where reading becomes engaging, productive, and accessible for everyone.

TIPS AND TRICKS FOR MICROSOFT IMMERSIVE READER

Microsoft Immersive Reader is packed with features that make reading, comprehension, and communication more accessible. While the core functionalities like text customization and Read Aloud are straightforward, there are hidden gems and shortcuts that can further enhance your experience. This chapter will uncover these tips and tricks, empowering you to maximize Immersive Reader's potential.

1. Use Keyboard Shortcuts for Faster Navigation

Why It's Helpful:
Keyboard shortcuts save time and make navigating Immersive Reader more efficient, especially during tasks like reviewing lengthy documents or switching between features.

Top Shortcuts:

- **Tab Key:** Cycle through options like grammar tools, translation, and text preferences
- **Esc Key:** Exit Immersive Reader quickly.
- **Spacebar:** Start and stop Read Aloud.

Pro Tip: Combine these shortcuts with regular navigation to move seamlessly through documents.

2. Highlight Key Sections with Line Focus

Why It's Helpful:
Line focus is a simple yet powerful tool that helps you zero in on specific parts of text, minimizing distractions and improving comprehension.

Trick:

- Customize the focus to highlight one, three, or five lines at a time, depending on your reading preference.
- Combine line focus with Read Aloud to reinforce understanding.

Example: Sarah used the three-line focus setting to review an email with critical project updates, ensuring she didn't miss any details.

3. Use the Picture Dictionary for Quick Clarification

Why It's Helpful:
The Picture Dictionary provides visual context for words, making it especially useful for young learners or individuals encountering unfamiliar vocabulary.

Trick:

- Hover over a word to see an image that represents its meaning.
- Pair the Picture Dictionary with Read Aloud to hear the word pronounced while viewing the visual.

Example: Sarah's niece used Immersive Reader during her online homework to understand challenging vocabulary, making the learning process engaging and fun.

4. Translate Content in Real Time

Why It's Helpful:
Immersive Reader's translation feature enables seamless communication across languages, making it invaluable in global teams and multicultural classrooms.

Trick:

- Translate specific words by clicking on them, or switch the entire document to a different language in a single click.
- Use Read Aloud in the translated language to hear proper pronunciation.

Example: Sarah used Immersive Reader to translate a client report from English to Spanish, then sent the simplified version to her team for review.

5. Personalize the Text Display

Why It's Helpful:
Customizing text size, font, and background colors can significantly enhance readability, especially for users with visual impairments or reading difficulties.

Trick:

- Experiment with different background colors to reduce glare or visual strain.
- Use the "Comic Sans" font option, which is particularly effective for individuals with dyslexia.

Example: Sarah's colleague adjusted the background to a calming sepia tone, helping him focus on long technical documents without eye fatigue.

6. Maximize Accessibility in Teams

Why It's Helpful:
Immersive Reader's integration with Microsoft Teams makes it a powerful tool for improving communication and understanding in team settings.

Trick:

- Simplify long chat messages by activating Immersive Reader directly from the message menu.
- Use translation tools in Teams to ensure multilingual team members are included.

Example: During a team meeting, Sarah used Immersive Reader to translate a colleague's post from French, ensuring seamless collaboration.

7. Save and Share Enhanced Content

Why It's Helpful:
Sharing content processed through Immersive Reader ensures inclusivity and accessibility for everyone.

Trick:

- Save simplified or translated versions of documents for distribution.
- Use Immersive Reader during presentations to make content clearer for all attendees.

Example: Sarah prepared a client presentation by simplifying complex technical documents using Immersive Reader, then shared the polished version with her audience.

8. Pair Immersive Reader with Other Microsoft 365 Tools

Why It's Helpful:
Immersive Reader becomes even more powerful when combined with tools like OneNote, Word, and SharePoint.

Trick:

- Use Immersive Reader in OneNote to enhance your study materials or meeting notes.
- Simplify Word documents before uploading them to SharePoint for team collaboration.

Example: Sarah streamlined her team's workflow by creating accessible Word documents and sharing them through OneDrive, ensuring everyone could engage with the material.

9. Use Copilot to Enhance Immersive Reader

Why It's Helpful:
Integrating Copilot with Immersive Reader takes accessibility and productivity to the next level.

Trick:

- Ask Copilot to summarize content in simpler terms before using Immersive Reader for enhanced readability.
- Use Copilot to generate accessible formats of your documents for broader audiences.

Example: Sarah combined Copilot and Immersive Reader to simplify a dense industry report, turning it into an easy-to-understand summary for her team.

10. Explore Read Aloud Voices and Speeds

Why It's Helpful:
Personalizing the Read Aloud feature can make listening more engaging and suited to your pace.

Trick:

- Experiment with different voice options to find one that's most comfortable for you.
- Adjust the speed to match your listening preference—slower for detailed comprehension, faster for scanning.

Example: While multitasking during a busy day, Sarah used Read Aloud at a higher speed to absorb the key points of an article without pausing her work.

These tips and tricks are designed to help you uncover Immersive Reader's full potential. Whether you're using it for personal learning, professional productivity, or educational support, the possibilities are endless.

A SMARTER WAY TO READ AND UNDERSTAND

Imagine having a personal assistant that not only enhances your reading experience but also helps you digest, summarize, and translate content effortlessly. That's exactly what Microsoft Copilot brings to Immersive Reader—a seamless integration of artificial intelligence (AI) that empowers you to read smarter, faster, and more effectively.

In this chapter, we'll dive into how Copilot works with Immersive Reader, exploring the ways it can transform how you interact with text, overcome challenges, and achieve your goals.

Copilot in Immersive Reader is an AI-powered tool designed to enhance your reading experience by providing contextual support and actionable insights. Think of it as a digital reading companion that adapts to your needs. Whether you're deciphering dense documents, translating text, or breaking down complex language, Copilot steps in to make the process intuitive and efficient.

Key Features of Copilot in Immersive Reader

1. **Content Summarization**
    - Quickly generate summaries of lengthy or complex documents.
    - Focus on key points without losing the context.

Example: Sarah received a 20-page technical report. By asking Copilot, "Summarize this document," she instantly had a concise overview, saving hours of reading time.

Pro Tip: Use Copilot's summaries as a starting point, then dive into Immersive Reader for deeper analysis.

2. **Simplification of Text**
    - Rewrite dense paragraphs into simpler, more readable language.
    - Adjust complexity levels based on your preferences.

Example: Struggling with legal jargon in a contract, Sarah prompted Copilot to simplify the text, making it easier to understand.

Pro Tip: Combine text simplification with Immersive Reader's grammar tools to reinforce comprehension.

3. **Language Translation and Localization**
    - Translate text seamlessly while retaining cultural and linguistic nuances.
    - Access Read Aloud in the translated language for pronunciation support.

Example: During a global project, Sarah used Copilot to translate a German document into English, then leveraged Immersive Reader's Read Aloud feature to understand the translated content.

Pro Tip: Ask Copilot to translate idiomatic phrases for a more accurate understanding of localized expressions.

4. **Highlighting Key Themes**
    - Identify recurring themes, keywords, or concepts within a text.
    - Use visual highlights to focus on important sections.

Example: Sarah analyzed meeting notes using Copilot, which flagged critical action items and highlighted decisions made during the discussion.

Pro Tip: Combine this feature with line focus in Immersive Reader for targeted reading.

5. **Generating Questions and Insights**
    - Ask Copilot questions about the text to clarify confusing sections.
    - Use AI-generated insights to gain a deeper understanding of the material.

Example: Sarah didn't understand a section of a technical paper. She typed, "Explain this paragraph," and Copilot provided a detailed breakdown.

Pro Tip: Use Copilot's questions to test your understanding of educational materials or prepare for presentations.

How to Use Copilot with Immersive Reader

Using Copilot with Immersive Reader is straightforward. Here's how to get started:

1. **Activate Copilot:** Open a supported document or message, then click the Copilot icon to launch the AI assistant.
2. **Combine Features:** Use Copilot alongside Immersive Reader's text preferences, grammar tools, and Read Aloud to customize your experience.
3. **Ask Questions:** Type natural language prompts, like "Summarize this," "Translate to Spanish," or "Highlight key points," and let Copilot handle the rest.

Best Practices for Copilot in Immersive Reader

- **Be Specific:** The more detailed your prompts, the better Copilot can tailor its responses to your needs.

- **Iterate and Refine:** Don't hesitate to ask follow-up questions or request alternative summaries for clarity.
- **Pair Features Strategically:** Use Copilot for summarization and translation, then rely on Immersive Reader's tools for grammar and focus adjustments.
- **Learn as You Go:** Examine how Copilot simplifies or translates text to improve your own skills over time.

Real-World Applications of Copilot in Immersive Reader

1. **In Education:** Teachers can simplify dense texts for students or generate discussion questions on the fly.
2. **In the Workplace:** Professionals can quickly analyze reports, translate emails, and prepare summaries for team discussions.
3. **For Personal Growth:** Language learners can combine Copilot's translation and grammar insights to enhance vocabulary and comprehension.

Example: Sarah used Copilot to simplify a policy document for her team, then applied Immersive Reader to highlight key responsibilities. This approach saved time and improved understanding across her group.

With Copilot, Microsoft Immersive Reader becomes an even more powerful tool for productivity and accessibility. By combining AI-driven insights with customizable reading features, you can tackle even the most challenging texts with confidence.

COMMON PITFALLS AND HOW TO AVOID THEM

While Immersive Reader is a powerful tool for enhancing comprehension and accessibility, like any technology, it comes with potential pitfalls that can hinder its effectiveness if not addressed. This chapter identifies common challenges users encounter when using Immersive Reader and provides practical solutions to help you avoid them.

1. Relying Too Much on Automation

The Pitfall:
Immersive Reader's automation features, like Read Aloud and translation, are incredibly helpful but can lead to over-reliance. This might result in a lack of engagement with the material or missed nuances in the text.

Why It Happens:
The ease of letting the tool handle tasks can discourage deeper interaction with the content.

How to Avoid It:

- Use automation as a supplement, not a replacement, for active reading.
- Pair tools like Read Aloud with line focus to stay engaged while listening.
- Cross-check translations or summaries for accuracy and context.

Example: Sarah used Copilot to summarize a technical report but still reviewed the details manually to ensure nothing critical was omitted.

2. Misinterpreting Translations

The Pitfall:
Immersive Reader's translation feature is excellent, but it's not perfect. Misinterpretations can occur, especially with idiomatic phrases or highly technical language.

Why It Happens:
Translation algorithms may struggle with context-specific meanings or nuanced expressions.

How to Avoid It:

- Use the Picture Dictionary and context clues to validate translations.
- Ask Copilot follow-up questions about unclear phrases.
- When in doubt, consult a human translator for critical documents.

Example: While reviewing a translated client email, Sarah noticed a phrase didn't make sense. She rephrased her query to Copilot, which provided a clearer interpretation.

3. Overlooking Customization Options

The Pitfall:
Some users dive into Immersive Reader without adjusting text size, background colors, or grammar tools, missing out on features that could greatly enhance their experience.

Why It Happens:
New users may not explore the full range of customization settings.

How to Avoid It:

- Spend time experimenting with text preferences and other settings.

- Adjust settings based on the type of content you're reading (e.g., larger fonts for dense text, calming colors for lengthy documents).

Example: Sarah struggled with a visually overwhelming document until she adjusted the background to sepia and increased line spacing, making the text more approachable.

4. Skipping Grammar Tools

The Pitfall:
Features like syllable splitting and parts of speech highlighting are often underutilized, especially by advanced readers who don't think they need them.

Why It Happens:
Users may assume grammar tools are only for beginners or language learners.

How to Avoid It:

- Try grammar tools even if you're a confident reader—they can help with complex texts or unfamiliar terms.
- Use these tools to analyze technical documents or learn new vocabulary.

Example: Sarah used parts of speech highlighting to better understand a legal document, improving her grasp of its structure.

5. Ignoring Accessibility Features in Teams

The Pitfall:
When using Immersive Reader in Teams, users might overlook features like line focus or translation, leading to miscommunication during team discussions.

Why It Happens:
The focus on collaboration can overshadow the tool's accessibility features.

How to Avoid It:

- Use Immersive Reader to simplify and translate messages in Teams chats.
- Highlight key sections of posts or notes to ensure clarity during meetings.

Example: Sarah enabled Immersive Reader during a team brainstorming session to ensure she fully understood a colleague's technical explanation in a different language.

6. Underestimating the Value of Copilot

The Pitfall:
Some users may not fully explore how Copilot enhances Immersive Reader, missing out on features like contextual summaries or tailored insights.

Why It Happens:
A lack of familiarity with Copilot's capabilities can prevent users from taking full advantage of its integration.

How to Avoid It:

- Experiment with Copilot prompts like "Summarize this text" or "Highlight key points."
- Combine Copilot's insights with Immersive Reader's tools for a deeper understanding of the material.

Example: Sarah initially only used Copilot for translation but later discovered its ability to simplify reports, saving her significant time.

7. Failing to Review AI-Generated Content

The Pitfall:
Users may blindly trust summaries or translations generated by Immersive Reader and Copilot without verifying their accuracy.

Why It Happens:
The convenience of automation can lead to assumptions that the output is always correct.

How to Avoid It:

- Cross-check AI-generated summaries with the original text.
- Use Copilot's follow-up functionality to refine summaries or clarifications.

Example: Sarah reviewed a Copilot-generated summary of a financial report and identified a missed nuance, ensuring her analysis was complete.

8. Overcomplicating Simple Tasks

The Pitfall:
Some users might use advanced features unnecessarily, making simple tasks more complex than they need to be.

Why It Happens:
Excitement about the tool's capabilities can lead to overuse.

How to Avoid It:

- Match the tool's features to the task at hand. For simple documents, basic settings may suffice.
- Reserve advanced tools for more complex or detailed work.

Example: Sarah simplified a short email with Read Aloud rather than applying grammar tools and translation features she didn't need.

Avoiding these pitfalls ensures you get the most out of Microsoft Immersive Reader without frustration or wasted effort. By using this tool thoughtfully and strategically, you can unlock its full potential to support your reading and productivity needs.

SARAH'S JOURNEY WITH IMMERSIVE READER

The afternoon sunlight streamed through the windows of Sarah's home office, where she sat staring at a dense, jargon-filled report from her company's global team. The document was over 30 pages long, written in a mix of English and French, and Sarah had been tasked with summarizing the key points for her next team meeting.

Her initial reaction was panic. Sarah wasn't fluent in French, and the English sections were loaded with technical terms she wasn't familiar with. The deadline loomed, and her usual approach—tediously breaking the content down line by line—wasn't going to cut it this time.

As she searched for a way to simplify her task, Sarah remembered a colleague mentioning Microsoft Immersive Reader during a recent training session. Curious, she opened the report in Word Online, clicked on the View tab, and selected Immersive Reader.

The transformation was immediate. The cluttered document turned into a clean, streamlined layout with larger text and wider spacing. She adjusted the background to a calming sepia tone, reducing her eye strain. For the first time, the report didn't feel as overwhelming.

Sarah decided to try the Read Aloud feature. A clear, professional voice began narrating the text, helping her focus on the content without getting bogged down by the dense formatting. She increased the playback speed slightly to match her reading pace, allowing her to absorb the material quickly.

When she reached the French sections, Sarah was at a standstill. Then she remembered Immersive Reader's translation feature. She clicked on the Translate option, selected English as her preferred language, and watched as the French text transformed into clear, readable English.

To ensure accuracy, Sarah asked Copilot to explain any phrases that still felt unclear. For example, a translated idiom didn't make sense in

English, but Copilot rephrased it with a more culturally appropriate meaning.

"It's like having a personal language coach," she thought, marveling at how quickly she could now work through multilingual content.

The English sections of the report weren't much easier, filled with technical jargon about financial modeling. To make sense of it, Sarah turned on Grammar Tools, highlighting nouns, verbs, and adjectives in different colors. This broke the text into digestible chunks, helping her identify the key players and actions in each paragraph.

Next, she used Copilot to summarize the report. "What are the three most important points in this document?" she typed. Copilot delivered a concise summary, pinpointing trends in the data and the main recommendations from the team.

Still, Sarah wanted to ensure her team would understand her findings. She activated Immersive Reader's Line Focus feature to review the document line by line, double-checking for details she might have missed.

With the report broken down into manageable pieces, Sarah moved on to her next task: preparing a presentation for her team. She used Immersive Reader's Picture Dictionary to clarify a few remaining terms, ensuring she could explain them clearly to her colleagues.

To save time, Sarah asked Copilot to create a bullet-point summary of the report's highlights. It generated a list of action items, which she polished and integrated into her slides.

During the meeting, Sarah's confidence was evident. She explained the report's key findings clearly, answered her colleagues' questions, and even shared how Immersive Reader had helped her navigate the complexities of the document.

As Sarah closed her laptop at the end of the day, she felt a sense of accomplishment. What had initially seemed like an impossible task had become a manageable and even rewarding experience. Immersive Reader had not only simplified her workflow but also expanded her capabilities—bridging language gaps, breaking down technical content, and giving her the confidence to tackle future challenges.

Sarah's story is a reminder that even the most daunting tasks can be overcome with the right tools. Immersive Reader, paired with Copilot, transforms the way we interact with text, turning barriers into opportunities for growth.

What challenges could Immersive Reader help you overcome? Whether it's simplifying complex documents, learning a new language, or making your workflow more efficient, the possibilities are endless.

IMMERSIVE READER AND YOUR JOURNEY

As we conclude our exploration of Microsoft Immersive Reader, it's time to reflect on what we've learned and how these insights can transform your reading and comprehension journey. Immersive Reader is more than a tool—it's a bridge to understanding, accessibility, and connection. Whether you're a student, professional, or lifelong learner, this feature empowers you to engage with text on your terms.

Summary of Key Insights

1. **What is Immersive Reader?**
   Immersive Reader is a dynamic, accessible tool that adapts to your unique reading needs. Its features—like Read Aloud, text customization, grammar tools, and translation—make text more approachable and engaging for all users, regardless of their abilities or challenges.

2. **Why Use Immersive Reader?**
   By enhancing focus, breaking down language barriers, and fostering inclusivity, Immersive Reader supports productivity, collaboration, and learning. Its versatility benefits students mastering complex material, professionals navigating dense documents, and anyone seeking a more personalized reading experience.

3. **Getting Started and Best Practices**
   From enabling line focus to customizing text preferences, the key to mastering Immersive Reader lies in tailoring it to your needs. Pairing its features with other Microsoft tools—like OneNote, Word, or Teams—can amplify its impact.

4. **Tips and Tricks**
   Unlocking the full potential of Immersive Reader involves

exploring its lesser-known features. Tools like the Picture Dictionary and Copilot integration elevate its capabilities, making it an indispensable part of your workflow.

5. **Avoiding Common Pitfalls**
   Using Immersive Reader thoughtfully—by cross-checking translations, balancing automation with engagement, and saving content for collaboration—ensures a seamless and impactful experience.

6. **Copilot and Immersive Reader**
   The integration of AI through Copilot brings a new dimension to Immersive Reader. From summarizing content to simplifying jargon and translating seamlessly, Copilot complements Immersive Reader's features, making even the most complex tasks approachable.

Sarah's story exemplifies the transformative potential of Immersive Reader. Faced with a daunting task—a multilingual, jargon-heavy report—Sarah initially felt overwhelmed. But by leveraging Immersive Reader's features, she turned a challenge into an opportunity for growth.

- **Empowering Accessibility:** Sarah's use of translation tools and grammar highlights reflects how Immersive Reader can break down barriers, enabling clearer communication and understanding.

- **Building Confidence:** As Sarah explored features like line focus and Read Aloud, she became more confident in her ability to manage complex content. This mirrors how readers can develop their own skills by engaging with Immersive Reader.

- **Enhancing Collaboration:** By simplifying and translating content, Sarah not only improved her own comprehension but also facilitated collaboration with her team, demonstrating how Immersive Reader fosters inclusivity and teamwork.

Your journey may not look exactly like Sarah's, but the lessons are universal. Immersive Reader is here to adapt to your needs, making learning, reading, and collaboration more accessible and efficient.

As you reflect on the content of this book, think about how Immersive Reader can fit into your daily life. What challenges could it help you overcome? How can its features enhance your productivity, communication, or personal growth?

Remember, Immersive Reader is just one tool in the vast Microsoft ecosystem. It pairs seamlessly with other apps like Teams, SharePoint, and OneNote, creating endless possibilities for innovation and collaboration.

Like Sarah, you have the power to transform how you interact with text. Immersive Reader isn't just about reading—it's about understanding, growing, and connecting in ways that matter.

UNLOCKING YOUR POTENTIAL WITH IMMERSIVE READER

As we close this exploration of Microsoft Immersive Reader, take a moment to reflect on how far you've come. Immersive Reader isn't just a tool—it's a key to transformation. It empowers you to read, learn, and communicate more effectively, bridging gaps and breaking barriers. Whether you're overcoming personal challenges, collaborating with global teams, or exploring new ways to grow, Immersive Reader offers the flexibility and innovation you need to succeed.

Throughout this book, we've seen how Immersive Reader can turn obstacles into opportunities:

- It makes content more accessible, ensuring that everyone—regardless of their abilities—can engage meaningfully with text.
- It fosters productivity by streamlining complex tasks, from breaking down technical documents to translating multilingual content.
- It promotes collaboration by creating an inclusive environment where everyone's voice can be understood.

But most importantly, it encourages you to think differently about how you approach learning and communication.

Immersive Reader is just one piece of the Microsoft 365 ecosystem, a suite of tools designed to work together seamlessly. Its integration with apps like Teams, Word, and OneNote ensures that you can carry its benefits across all aspects of your work and life.

Imagine:

- Using Immersive Reader in Teams to enhance real-time collaboration.
- Leveraging its features in OneNote to create more engaging study materials.

- Pairing it with SharePoint to make shared content accessible for everyone.

These connections amplify the possibilities, making your workflow smoother, your communication clearer, and your productivity limitless.

Technology evolves constantly, and so does the way we use it. Immersive Reader is continually updated with new features and improvements, ensuring it remains a cutting-edge resource for accessibility and productivity.

Your journey with Microsoft tools doesn't end here. Immersive Reader is part of a broader world of innovation within the Microsoft 365 ecosystem. By continuing to explore these tools, you'll discover new ways to enhance your skills, connect with others, and achieve your goals.

This book is just one chapter in a larger story. The Microsoft 365 Companion Series is designed to help you master other tools like Word, Teams, OneNote, and more, each offering its unique set of features and opportunities. These books provide the same conversational, approachable guidance you've experienced here, helping you unlock the full potential of Microsoft 365.

Whether you're diving deeper into collaboration with Teams, enhancing productivity with Excel, or exploring creative tools like Sway, there's always something new to learn.

As you turn the last page, remember that Immersive Reader—and the entire Microsoft 365 ecosystem—is here to support your growth. Your journey is unique, and these tools are designed to adapt to your needs, helping you succeed in ways that matter most to you.

So go forward with confidence. Experiment with features, explore new tools, and share your knowledge with others. The possibilities are endless, and the power to transform your learning, productivity, and communication is right at your fingertips.

Thank you for embarking on this journey with Immersive Reader. Here's to many more discoveries ahead!

www.ingramcontent.com/pod-product-compliance
Lightning Source LLC
Chambersburg PA
CBHW070940220526
45469CB00007B/2456